purchase 6/04

LONG PASSAGE TO KOREA

BLACK SAILORS AND THE INTEGRATION OF THE U.S. NAVY

Bernard C. Nalty

THE U.S. NAVY AND THE KOREAN WAR

EDWARD J. MAROLDA
SERIES EDITOR

NAVAL HISTORICAL CENTER
DEPARTMENT OF THE NAVY
WASHINGTON 2003

Cover design by Morgan I. Wilbur
Book design by John A. Grier

Library of Congress Cataloging-in-Publication Data

Nalty, Bernard C.
    Long passage to Korea : Black sailors and the integration of the U.S. Navy / Bernard
C. Nalty.
      p. cm. — (The U.S. Navy and the Korean War)
    Includes bibliographical references.
    ISBN 0-945274-48-3 (alk. paper)
      1. United States. Navy—African Americans. 2. African American sailors. 3. Korean
War, 1950-1953—Participation, African American. I. Title. II. Series.

    VB324.A47N35 2003
    359'.008996'073—dc21   2003042178

For sale by the Superintendent of Documents, U.S. Government Printing Office
Internet: bookstore.gpo.gov Phone: toll free (866) 512-1800; DC area (202) 512-1800
Fax: (202) 512-2250 Mail: Stop SSOP, Washington, DC 20402-0001

ISBN 0-16-051355-3

Contents

Portrayed in the cockpit of his F4U-4 Corsair, Ensign Jesse L. Brown was the first African American naval aviator to serve in combat. The young officer was a member of Fighter Squadron 32 based on board carrier Leyte *(CV 32) off the east coast of North Korea. On 4 December 1950, while flying a mission in support of the 1st Marine Division near the Chosin Reservoir, Brown was forced to crash-land his disabled plane in mountainous terrain. Despite heroic efforts, Brown's wingman could not free the injured and dying pilot from the wrecked aircraft. Oil portrait by Clifford Lee.*

Foreword

THIS MONOGRAPH, THE THIRD in the Naval Historical Center's series commemorating the Korean War, not only covers the contribution of African American Sailors in that conflict but traces the story of racial integration in the U.S. Navy since the American Revolution. During the early republic, when the fledgling navy needed seamen of all colors to protect the nation, African Americans were part of every warship's crew. In the Civil War, African Americans fought with distinction in ironclads on the Mississippi, in blockading vessels on the East and Gulf coasts, and in warships patrolling the oceans of the world. Growing racial polarization in American society in the late 19th and early 20th centuries, however, affected the status of African American Sailors who were excluded from most shipboard billets and limited to the less desired ratings, such as stewards and coal heavers.

Political action by black and white Americans to end racial injustice in the armed forces, the manpower demands of a nation fighting for survival, and the realization that the United States could not condemn Nazi and Japanese racism abroad while condoning it at home led to some changes in the Navy's racial policies during World War II. Not until the early Cold War years did the nation squarely face the issue of racial integration of the armed forces. Both to right a historic wrong and to make political capital, on 26 July 1948, President Harry S. Truman issued Executive Order 9981 that established a policy of equal treatment and opportunity for all military members.

Racial inequality would continue to plague the Navy and the other armed forces for many more years to come, but during the Korean War of 1950–1953, black and white Sailors and Marines fought side by side once again. African Americans piloted fighters and attack aircraft, manned guns on board battleships, cruisers, and destroyers, and fought their way up and down the hard, cold hills of Korea. Black women continued their service in the Navy Nurse Corps and in the regular Navy. Lieutenant (jg) Jesse Brown and many other African Americans paid the ultimate price while doing their duty for the country. We are fortunate that Bernard Nalty, a renowned authority on racial integration of the armed services, has completed this fine study. His familiarity with the relevant issues, as well as with the best primary and secondary sources, makes this social history especially valuable to the Sailors and Marines who now defend the nation.

Several individuals are responsible for the success of this series and deserve special recognition: Dr. Edward J. Marolda, Senior Historian of the Naval Historical Center and the series editor; Ms. Sandra Doyle, the Center's Senior Editor; Lieutenant Colonel Steven Held, USMC, the Navy–Marine Corps Korean War Commemoration Coordinator, and his predecessor Lieutenant Colonel Ward E. Scott, USMC; the Naval Historical Foundation; and the Marine Corps History and Museums Division. As with all works in the series, the views expressed are those of the author and do not necessarily reflect those of the Department of the Navy or any other U.S. government agency.

William S. Dudley
Director of Naval History

Preface

THE KOREAN WAR, LIKE THE other conflicts in the nation's history, challenged the Navy to make the most efficient and effective use of its resources, both human and material. Throughout all of its wars, the recruiting, training, and assignment of African Americans posed a recurring problem for the U.S. government in the employment of manpower because of slavery and the racial discrimination it spawned. As early as the undeclared naval war with France, 1798–1800, the Navy of the United States tapped the reservoir of free black fishermen and merchant seamen then available in northern seaports. Reliance on racially integrated crews survived beyond the Civil War and the abolition of slavery, only to succumb to the principle of separate but equal, validated in 1896 by the Supreme Court. As racial segregation took hold and the era of Jim Crow began, the Navy separated blacks from whites, a task completed by the outbreak of World War I in 1917, and paid the price in lost efficiency to maintain the policy during that conflict and afterward. The unprecedented demands of World War II, however, created pressure for a more rational use of human resources that eroded but did not destroy racial segregation in the Navy.

Secretary of the Navy James V. Forrestal, who took office in 1944, concluded that the training and assignments available to African Americans had to reflect their abilities and the needs of the wartime Navy, instead of being determined almost exclusively by race. By the time the war ended, the Navy had commissioned its first black officers, experimented with a few ships manned by African Americans, and begun integrating the races in the crews of fleet auxiliaries like oilers and ammunition ships, though not on combat ships where the only African American Sailors continued to be cooks or stewards.

After World War II ended, racial integration lost the headway gained during the last year of the conflict. Japan's surrender in September 1945 triggered the headlong demobilization of the armed forces of the United States. Many of the ships that had helped win the war were mothballed or sacrificed in tests of the new atomic bomb. Crewmembers went home, the African Americans among them returning to experience the humiliations of a society where racial segregation still prevailed.

President Harry S. Truman challenged the existing racial policy on 26 July 1948, when he ordered the armed forces to integrate the races, but compliance proved uneven at best, with the Navy and Army lagging behind the newly established Air Force. When communist North Korea invaded South Korea on 25 June 1950, the smaller peacetime Navy had proportionally fewer African American Sailors than during World War II, and most of those still in uniform served in the Steward Branch where they performed housekeeping duties.

The outbreak of war in Korea launched another period of rapid growth for the Navy. The new recruits, reservists recalled to wartime active duty, and newly commissioned officers included African Americans who, thanks to the President's directive of July 1948, often received better treatment and greater opportunity in uniform than they had encountered as civilians. The new policy of racial integration was in place, as were the Navy Department directives to carry it out, but the naval service, despite its successful experience with racial integration as World War II ended, had not yet shaken off the dead hand of racism.

To its credit, the Navy that fought the Korean War made a determined effort to carry out President Truman's racial policy. This campaign had three major objectives: to increase the number of African Americans, especially officers but also enlisted men, and make full use of their abilities; to encourage black Sailors to choose specialties other than steward duty; and to mitigate the effects of racial segregation, which prevailed by law or custom throughout much of the nation, on the Navy's African Americans in their contacts with civilian society. During the Korean conflict, the Navy demonstrated a commitment to equal treatment and opportunity, regardless of race, that took root and flourishes today.

Bernard C. Nalty

Introduction

ON 4 DECEMBER 1950, the Iroquois Flight took off from the aircraft carrier *Leyte* (CV 33) to support U.S. Marines and soldiers then under fierce attack by Chinese troops in the snow-clad ridges and villages near the ice-covered Chosin (Changjin) Reservoir of northeastern Korea. Ensign Jesse L. Brown, one of the first African Americans to earn the gold wings of a Naval Aviator, piloted one of the six Vought F4U Corsairs in the flight. The formation crossed the North Korean coastline and searched for the enemy along the western shore of the reservoir, less than a thousand feet above the hostile terrain.

Near the abandoned village of Somong-ni, Lieutenant (jg) William H. Koenig saw vapor streaming from Brown's Corsair and radioed a warning. Koenig hoped that the plume resulted from a transfer of fuel from one tank to another, but Brown replied that he was rapidly losing fuel pressure and would have to crash-land.

Earlier that day, fire from the ground had damaged another F4U, and the pilot had chosen to make a belly-landing, a dangerous undertaking. Trying to land a damaged Corsair—some six tons of metal, ammunition, and volatile fuel—could be deadly. In this instance the attempt failed; when the aircraft hit the ground, it exploded, killing the pilot.

Brown nevertheless decided to risk a crash landing rather than parachute into the forbidding mountains. Lieutenant (jg) Thomas Hudner, his wingman, talked Brown through the check list for an emergency landing as the Corsair lost power and altitude and its pilot searched for a reasonably level piece of ground free of boulders or other large obstructions. Brown guided

In VF 32's ready room on board Leyte, *Ensign Jesse Brown and his squadron mates listen intently as an officer relays information about executing air operations over North Korea. The effectiveness of Navy and Marine Corps air support was critical to the survival of Marine and other allied ground forces during the harsh winter of 1950.*

A Marine Corsair drops a napalm bomb on Chinese Communist troops blocking the road ahead. Aircraft flown by Jesse Brown and other Navy and Marine pilots helped the 1st Marine Division fight its way to the coast of North Korea in December 1950.

the plane onto a snowy hillside, but as the Corsair skidded up a 20-degree slope, the fuselage broke just forward of the cockpit, pinning the pilot's right knee in a tangle of metal. Conscious but unable to free himself, Brown waved to the other members of the Iroquois Flight, signaling that he had survived.

As Hudner circled, he saw smoke rising from the shattered engine compartment and realized that the wreckage might burst into flame before a rescue helicopter could arrive. While the helicopter was en route to the site, Hudner decided to crash land on the hillside near Brown and try to put out the fire and free the injured aviator from the wreckage. The second Corsair slammed onto the snow and skidded on its belly to a safe stop about 100 yards from the trapped pilot. Brown stoically

endured the pain as Hudner struggled unsuccessfully to free him. The would-be rescuer could do little but use his gloved hands to scoop snow onto the source of the smoke, try to warm Brown with a scarf, and encourage the injured pilot to hold on until the helicopter reached them.

Ironically, Hudner's gallant attempt to save Brown had delayed the arrival of the rescue helicopter. The chopper pilot, Marine First Lieutenant Charlie Ward, knew that his aircraft could barely lift three persons—himself, his crew chief, and Brown—in the thin air a mile above sea level. Now Hudner would also have to be picked up. Ward had no choice but to return to his base and drop off both the crew chief and the heavy tool kit that the helicopter normally carried. Ward landed at the crash site without the tools and thus had no way

of cutting or prying apart the metal that trapped the pilot. Brown asked Hudner and Ward to amputate his leg, but they did not have a saw or a knife that could sever bone. Eventually Brown lapsed into unconsciousness from his injuries and the bitter cold. All they could do was stay with Brown until he died. Unable even to remove his body, they flew off into the gathering darkness.

Hudner's rescue attempt earned him the Medal of Honor, awarded by President Harry S. Truman. A white pilot had risked his life to save a fellow aviator whom he respected and liked—a fellow pilot who happened to be black. Reality thus reversed a story line at the time often favored by Hollywood scriptwriters—the loyal African American willing to risk his life to save the white hero.

The Early Republic

AS IN KOREA, BLACK and white Sailors have often fought side by side, but the road to full equality for African Americans, which began in the early days of the U.S. Navy, proved long and tortuous. During the American Revolution, African Americans served in the Continental Navy, in the state navies, and on privateers. Blacks from Maryland and Virginia, free men and slaves, proved especially helpful to the revolutionary cause. Their familiarity with the Chesapeake Bay and its tributaries enabled them to serve as pilots or skippers, taking small craft where few others dared to go.

Despite the varied and extensive contributions of African Americans, the new United States Navy, when it emerged in 1798 from the control of the War Department, barred "Negroes or Mulatoes" from enlisting. The Marine Corps adopted the same ban, though allowing black civilian drummers or fifers to attract whites to the recruiting rendezvous.

The Marine Corps retained its prohibition until World War II. Because of its small size, the Corps could be more selective than the Navy. Moreover, the role of Marines in maintaining order and discipline on board ship and at shore installations enabled the organization to invoke the belief—which achieved the status of folk wisdom—that white men would not take orders from blacks. Not until 1942 did changing attitudes toward race in American society and the demands of the greatest war in the nation's history at last prod the Marine

Artist V. Zveg's oil painting "First Fleet Operation of the Continental Navy" portrays the new navy's 3 March 1776 amphibious landing on New Providence Island in the Bahamas. From the American Revolution to the present, African American Sailors have been an integral part of the U.S. Navy and have fought in all the nation's wars.

NH 79419-KN

The Impressment of Black Sailors

GREAT BRITAIN, FIGHTING a long and costly war against Napoleon in the early years of the 19th century, invoked the time-honored practice of impressment to man its Royal Navy ships. At first the British sent press gangs to grog shops and brothels, as was the custom, but eventually stopped foreign ships on the high seas and took off any seaman who was a British subject or, all too often, could not prove that he was not. This affront to the newly independent United States angered American Sailors, black and white.

In 1807, the British warship *Leopard* hailed the American frigate *Chesapeake* and demanded permission to search for deserters. The American captain refused, but he could fire only one shot for honor before British cannon killed three Sailors, wounded another eighteen, and forced him to strike his colors. The British took off four men who claimed American citizenship, including Daniel Martin, a black Sailor from West Port, Massachusetts. Only one of the four men was definitely a British subject. Five years later, Martin and one of the other men were returned to *Chesapeake* in Boston Harbor; the fourth died during his service in the Royal Navy. The *Chesapeake* incident was not the only such occurrence involving African Americans, at least ten of whom were impressed into the Royal Navy from merchant ships. Two of the victims were freed by the frigate *Constitution* as a result of her victories over the British warships *Java* and *Guerrierre* in the War of 1812, caused in part by the issue of impressment.

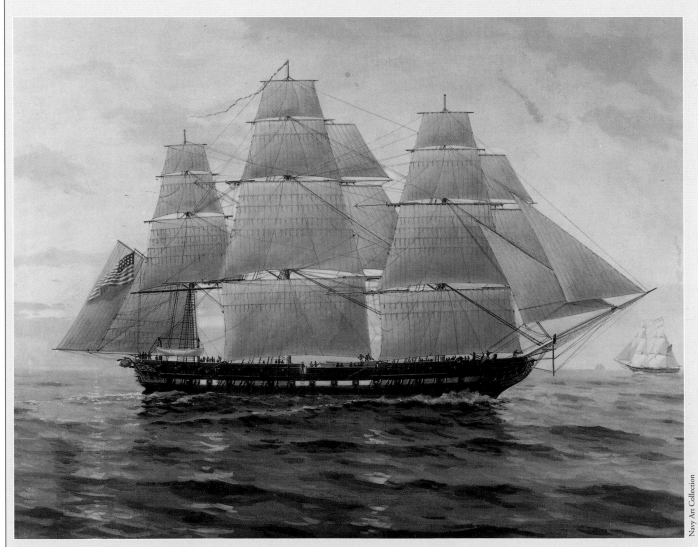

Navy Art Collection

"USS Chesapeake" by Francis Muller. In 1807 the British warship HMS Leopard *fired on USS* Chesapeake, *killing three men. The attackers then boarded the American naval vessel and removed four men, including an African American bluejacket, whom they claimed were subjects of the British king. The incident inflamed American opinion and contributed to the outbreak of war between the United States and Great Britain in 1812.*

Corps into accepting African Americans.

In contrast, the ink had barely dried on the directive excluding blacks when the Navy found it necessary to recruit them. The reluctance among white Americans to endure the rigors of the naval service—harsh discipline, long voyages, a monotonous diet, and the possibility of violent death or severe injury from accidents or combat—caused individual captains to ignore Navy Department policy and accept blacks. Although African American Sailors fought during the undeclared naval war with France, 1798–1800, they were not always welcome on board ship. Indeed, just three years after the fighting ended, Captain Edward Preble and other officers warned subordinates "not to Ship Black Men."

The War of 1812 caused the Navy to enlist openly and to accept officially free blacks, who were formally welcomed on board by an Act of Congress in March 1813. African Americans had fought on warships and privateers, on the high seas and the Great Lakes, before the law took effect, so the act merely brought policy into line with existing practice. For example, when the privateer *Governor Tompkins* clashed with a British man-of-war months before the legislation took effect, two African American Sailors, John Johnson and John Davis, suffered mortal wounds. While they clung to life, the men refused all aid so their shipmates would not have to abandon their posts to help them. The privateer's captain, Nathaniel Shaler, declared that "while America has such men, she has little to fear from the tyrants of the ocean."

The presence of black Sailors became a matter of routine. In 1816, two years after the signing of the treaty that ended the War of 1812, the surgeon of a typical American warship, *Java,* estimated that African Americans made up from one-eighth to one-sixth of the crew. Without free black Americans and foreign-born Sailors, the Navy could not have manned its sailing ships.

The victory of any American frigate against a hostile man-of-war inspired appreciation among civilians and increased the solidarity within crews. When a group of New Yorkers sought to express their thanks by inviting the crew of such a victorious warship to a stage performance, roughly half the men that marched into the theater were African Americans. Harmony did not always prevail, however, for when danger abated, friction sometimes arose between the races on board ship.

Although years of effective service earned free African Americans the right to enlist, the Navy Department took pains to make sure that no slaves served on shipboard. And for a time, neither free blacks nor slaves were employed as civilian workers at navy yards. White laborers opposed such hiring not only out of fear of competition from unpaid slaves or low-paid free blacks but also because of a belief in their own racial superiority.

NH 73971

This engraving depicts Commodore Thomas Macdonough, among his white and black shipmates, directing a ship's fire during the 11 September 1814 Battle of Lake Champlain. During the War of 1812, African Americans served in unskilled ratings (boy and landsman) and skilled ratings (ordinary seaman and able seaman) and in all theaters—the Great Lakes, the Atlantic, and the Gulf of Mexico.

Filling the Ranks

THE NAVY OPENLY accepted free blacks who demonstrated a willingness to reenlist at a time when few whites would join up, even though the presence of black seamen aroused the wrath of Southern slaveholders. In the 1830s, the most striking feature of the service may well have been the large number of blacks in its ranks. For example, an American traveling in Europe reported overhearing a conversation between two British tourists. They had concluded, after seeing American Sailors on liberty in Italy, that all Americans had black skin and that the white officers were recruited from the Royal Navy to exercise leadership. This perception reflected the Navy's continuing dependence on black Sailors.

Establishing a Racial Quota

Acting Secretary of the Navy Isaac Toucey paid attention to the concerns of Southern politicians, even though he had commanded black Sailors on the Great Lakes during the War of 1812, and established a quota on the recruitment of African Americans. They could not exceed 5 percent of the men enlisting. This policy did not specifically address reenlistment and proved difficult to enforce in a time when communications moved at a leisurely pace and captains reigned supreme. The Navy's policy failed to satisfy people like South Carolina Senator John C. Calhoun, a champion of slavery and states rights. Calhoun tried to banish blacks from the naval service, except as servants or cooks, but his attempt failed because the Navy of this era needed black Sailors.

To placate Calhoun and his like-minded colleagues, Secretary of the Navy Abel P. Upshur promised in 1842 that African Americans would make up no more than "one-twentieth part of the crew of any vessel," a pledge that depended on the primitive personnel accounting tools then in use—pen, ink, ledger book, and letter. Although difficult to enforce, the quota succeeded in reducing the percentage of African American new recruits to the desired level— 4.2 percent in 1850 and 5.6 percent in 1860.

None of the African American bluejackets could advance from forecastle to wardroom. As the British travelers observed, all naval officers were white. A number of blacks, however, served as masters of merchantmen or whalers. Indeed, the presence of black skippers in southern ports like Charleston, South Carolina, triggered complaints from local officials. As early as 1821, William Wirt, Attorney General in the cabinet of President James Monroe, tried to bar African American masters from the coastal trade, explaining that they were not full citizens capable of executing the sworn statements required of a ship's captain. This legal opinion, which in effect restricted black skippers to whatever American ports would accept them and to whaling voyages, lasted until 1862; some 80 years would pass before the Navy commissioned its first black officers.

The Pool of Black Manpower Expands

After secessionists fired on Fort Sumter, South Carolina, on 12 April 1861 and the Civil War began, the United States Navy reacted by blockading the ports of the newly formed Confederate States of America.

Robert A. Smalls

THE LIST OF BLACK heroes of the Civil War begins with Robert Smalls, a slave who won his freedom and fought for the United States. Smalls served as pilot of the 300-ton side-wheel steamer *Planter*, which operated out of Charleston, South Carolina. Before dawn on 13 May 1862, while the white skipper and mate were ashore, Smalls and the African American crew fired the boiler, built up steam, and cast off. *Planter*—with nine men, five women, and three children on board—put out to sea. A blockading ship, *Onward*, intercepted her. The Union captain assured Smalls

In 1862 Harper's Weekly *ran this depiction of the Confederate steam-driven gunboat* Planter.

Robert Smalls, naval hero of the Civil War. In May 1862, Smalls took control of the Confederate gunboat Planter in Charleston harbor, brought his family and other slaves on board, and made a daring escape. He turned the boat over to a Union blockading squadron. Eventually, Smalls was put in charge of the Planter, which served the federal government. After the war, Smalls won election to the South Carolina legislature and then the U.S. House of Representatives.

that all those on board had earned their freedom and turned over the steamer, with six cannon on board, to Federal authorities. For seizing the ship and weapons, Congress passed legislation that awarded some $4,500 in prize money; Smalls received the largest share, about $1,500.

Planter entered the service of the United States with Smalls as its master. Ill-suited for blockade operations, *Planter* plied the coastal waters delivering cargo for the U.S. Army quartermaster department and sometimes landing troops. Smalls was eventually commissioned as an officer of the Army's U.S. Colored Troops. In January 1865, while the steamer was undergoing repair in Philadelphia, Smalls encountered Northern racism. When he boarded a trolley in the city, a

conductor ordered him off. This insulting treatment of a war hero pricked the conscience of the city's leaders, who within two years ended the color bar on the city's transit system.

After the war, during the brief time that freed blacks dominated Southern politics, Smalls served in the state legislature of South Carolina and then as the state's representative in the U.S. House of Representatives. He also served as a major general in the South Carolina militia, until resurgent whites expelled blacks from positions of authority. During World War II, African American Sailors trained at Camp Robert Smalls, a facility named in honor of the black hero, at the Great Lakes Naval Training Station, near Chicago, Illinois. Reflecting the times, the camp was segregated.

African American Sailors served with the blockading squadrons in the Atlantic and on the Gulf Coast. Closing the ports formed only one part of a Union strategy to isolate and crush the Confederacy. Operations ashore liberated thousands of slaves and encouraged still others to flee to Union-controlled territory. These men formed a vast pool of manpower to perform labor and, with appropriate training, to fight.

As early as September 1861, Secretary of the Navy Gideon Welles authorized the enlistment of "contrabands"—escaped or liberated slaves. Initially, they could sign on only as "boys," normally lads under 18 years of age apprenticing to become Sailors, but, after December 1862, they could enlist as landsmen, able-bodied adults without nautical experience. A boy received between $8 and $10 each month, and a landsman earned $12, four dollars less than a seaman.

The reservoir of contrabands proved especially important in the fighting on the Mississippi River and some of its tributaries, where the Navy in October 1862 assumed control of operations from the War Department. Acting Rear Admiral David Dixon Porter arranged for the conversion of river steamboats to armored gunboats, creating a force of a hundred warships. To help man them, he began recruiting former slaves. These men were readily available, accustomed to hard labor, and, he believed, naturally resistant to the illnesses that had hospitalized some 400 white Sailors

"Hauling Down the Flag—Surrender of the Alabama *to the* Kearsarge *off Cherbourg, France, 19 June 1864" by J. O. Davidson. Union Sailors cheer but prepare to continue fighting as they witness the sinking of the Confederate raider CSS* Alabama *off Cherbourg. Throughout the 19th century, but especially during the Civil War, a significant number of African Americans served in the Navy. The Navy employed both free men and "contraband" slaves for the common purpose of ending America's "peculiar institution" and defeating the Confederacy.*

before the gunboat flotilla became ready for action.

Admiral Porter predicted a financial windfall for the Navy by recruiting contrabands. He advised the department that the substitution of lower-ranking blacks, either boys or landsmen, for higher-paid white seamen, especially in the engine rooms of the gunboats, could save exactly $112,608. Secretary of the Navy Welles put a crimp in this plan, however. He approved the enlistment of former slaves as landsmen and also agreed that a commanding officer might do what Porter recommended: employ them as ordinary seamen, seamen, firemen, or coalheavers, instead of their usual bluewater duty as shipboard laborers or officers' servants. Welles eliminated

NH 79929 from *Deeds of Valor* 2:70.

A few former slaves, or "contrabands," served the Union cause above and beyond the call of duty. For exceptional heroism during the Battle of Mobile Bay as an ammunition handler on board Admiral David Farragut's flagship, USS Hartford, *Landsman John Lawson earned the Congressional Medal of Honor.*

NH 60873

Racially integrated crews were the norm for USS Miami *and most other warships of the Union Navy.*

the projected savings when he directed that the African American landsmen assigned to the work that Porter described receive pay appropriate to the new duties. For a landsman serving as a coal-heaver, the difference in pay amounted to six dollars each month. Although prohibiting the transfer of contrabands from one vessel to another except in the grade of landsman, the secretary decreed that when the enlistments of the former slaves expired they would be discharged in the highest grade attained.

The recruiting of freed slaves swelled the number of African Americans in the wartime Navy. Until recently, historians have had difficulty arriving at reliable statistics on the number of African American Sailors. An estimate made in 1902 suggested that African Americans might have accounted for 30,000 of the 120,000 men who enlisted during the Civil War. The African American Sailors Project cosponsored by the Naval Historical Center, the National Park Service, and Howard University has identified 20,000 black Sailors by name. The program has also documented that African Americans served on an integrated basis on board nearly all of the Union's 700 naval vessels.

In "An August Morning with Farragut," artist William H. Overend captures the fury of naval combat at close quarters for the white and black Sailors of USS Hartford.

From Slavery to Jim Crow

THE DEFEAT OF THE Confederacy and the abolition of slavery in the United States ended forever the need for the Navy to patrol off the coast of Africa to prevent the importation of slaves, a mission first undertaken in 1843. Tensions with Great Britain, America's foe during the American Revolution and War of 1812, abated after the Civil War, so no potential enemy appeared on the horizon. The fleet would have to shrink. As the U.S. Navy declined in strength, the service needed fewer African Americans in its ranks. The proportion of blacks in the enlisted ranks fell from a maximum estimate of 20–25 percent during the Civil War to 13.1 percent in 1870.

These berth deck cooks in USS Ossipee, *a screw sloop of war, take time out from meal preparations to pose for this 1887 photo.*

Crewmen of the ill-fated battleship USS Maine *were captured on camera some time before an internal explosion destroyed the naval vessel in Havana, Cuba, then a Spanish colony. U.S. suspicion that Spain had ordered an attack on the American warship helped spark a war between the two countries. Of the 262 officers and men who died as a result of the February 1898 explosion, 22 were African Americans.*

The Navy, moreover, played no role in Reconstruction, the re-incorporation of the states of the former Confederacy into the Union, which proved the dominant political and social issue of the postwar years. As North and South came together, the Republican Party, with roots in the anti-slavery movement, lost its ardor for black freedom.

A wave of racism, fueled by competition for jobs between free blacks and white immigrants, swept the North after the Civil War. When the United States in 1876 celebrated the centennial of its independence, African American laborers were barred from working on the buildings in Philadelphia that housed the event. At the same time, the states of the South established the share-cropper system, which reduced African Americans living there to a

Even though strict racial segregation characterized society in the nation's capital during the early 1900s, African Americans held many important jobs at the Washington Navy Yard's Naval Gun Factory, as they had throughout the 19th century.

status similar to the slavery that the 13th Amendment had abolished.

The resurgence of racism caused some northern states to ignore laws enacted to protect the rights of African Americans. Meanwhile southern states instituted the "black codes," written and unwritten laws designed to keep blacks in their place and remind them that they were not equal to whites. "Jim Crow," the personification of this latest example of racism, impeded or reversed the social, economic, educational, and political gains that blacks had made as a result of the 13th, 14th, and 15th amendments to the Constitution. These amendments put an end to slavery and promised basic civil rights, regardless of race or previous servitude.

Jim Crow also affected the status of African Americans in the Navy. The number of black petty officers dwindled to a handful by 1870, and members of the race

American Sailors enjoy a sporting event in Great Britain during World War I. The separation of races was much less a factor in Europe than in the United States.

began gravitating from assignments that required seamen skills to those usually performed by landsmen, like cooking and cleaning up or waiting on officers.

Whites enlisting in the Navy brought with them the hardening attitude toward African Americans, and white Sailors no longer willingly slung hammocks alongside blacks or ate beside them. Looking back on his service in the Navy, a white former Sailor declared that the presence of blacks on board ship had become "one of the most disagreeable features of the naval service." This experience, he predicted, would extinguish any spark of sympathy for the African American and thus demonstrate the wisdom of segregating the races. By the end of the 19th century, racism had taken firm root in every aspect of American life; indeed, racial segregation became the law of the land because of the Supreme Court's decision in *Plessy v. Ferguson* (1896), which enshrined the principle of separate but equal.

Like the racial attitudes of white America, the needs of the Navy

On numerous occasions before and after World War I, the United States deployed naval forces to the Caribbean and other regions of the globe to protect American interests and citizens threatened by political or social turmoil. Often, U.S. warships dispatched landing parties of Sailors and Marines, like these men from battleship New Jersey, *to trouble spots ashore.*

changed at the turn of the century. Sailing ships had placed a premium on the discipline, strength, and agility of its bluejackets. The new steam-driven battleships, with their larger crews, had different priorities, demanding of various crewmembers a working knowledge of electricity and optics, reciprocating engines or turbines, and wireless communication. Machines tended to compensate for physical strength and to some extent agility.

Moreover, instead of recruiting mainly at seaports, where large numbers of blacks had volunteered for the sailing Navy, the service now recruited nationwide. The Navy did not believe that African Americans could master the technical skills needed in the age of steam, steel, and electricity. Even if the Navy had not shared the common perception that whites were trainable and blacks were not, it needed too many men to risk alienating the white majority. Since white recruits often objected to serving alongside blacks, the Navy decided to segregate the races.

To make segregation work, the Navy selected specialties that blacks could perform while messing and sleeping separately from the rest of the crew. Many became messmen, a rating established in 1893, and operated as servants and housekeepers. The ranks of the messmen included John H. "Dick" Turpin, who barely escaped death when an internal explosion destroyed the battleship *Maine* in Havana harbor in 1898. Other African Americans, like Robert Penn, toiled in the heat of the engine room. He earned the Medal

As American society became increasingly segregated during the early decades of the 20th century, so too did the U.S. Navy. By the end of By World War I, most enlisted African American Sailors served as mess attendants, like these men from the submarine tender USS Bushnell *(AS 2).*

of Honor for risking death to shut down a leaking boiler in the battleship *Iowa* that was patrolling off the coast of Cuba during the

NH 79956 from Deeds of Valor 2:04

Fireman Second Class Robert Penn was awarded the Medal of Honor for heroism while responding to a fire room accident in battleship Iowa *off Santiago de Cuba during the Spanish-American War.*

Spanish-American War. A few African Americans retained the ratings they had earned before Jim Crow took hold in the Navy. Gunner's Mate John Jordan, for example, was in charge of the gun crew that fired the first shot at the Battle of Manila Bay, which broke Spanish naval power in the Philippines.

The Navy's Efforts to Maintain Racial Segregation

By the end of World War I, and during the two decades that followed, few blacks served in the Navy. Those who still wore the uniform tended to be mess attendants, though a few long-service petty officers, who had earned their rank years earlier with gun crews or in engine rooms, were serving out their final years before retiring. In June 1940, when Adolf Hitler's Germany was overrunning France, only 4,007 African Americans served in the Navy, most of them as messmen, though at least one chief petty officer remained on duty.

Although the United States had begun to rearm by 1940, the Navy still had no interest in recruiting blacks except for an expanding Messman Branch, later redesignated as the Steward Branch. For example, the service called for 4,700 volunteers in July of that year, but only 200 of them could be African

> ## "I am convinced that it is no kindness to negroes to thrust them upon men of the white race."
>
> —Secretary of the Navy Frank Knox

Americans. Secretary of the Navy Frank Knox ignored the efforts of persons outside the Navy, whether politicians or champions of civil rights for African Americans, to persuade the service to recruit additional blacks and use them for naval rather than housekeeping duties. Knox insisted that his actions were for the benefit of African Americans, sparing them the embarrassment of having to compete against whites on equal terms. "I am convinced," he wrote, "that it is no kindness to negroes to thrust them upon men of the white race."

The General Board of the Navy, which functioned like an advisory staff, suggested Knox respond to criticism of the Navy's racial policy by pointing out that "colored men are now enlisted in the messman branch . . . and given every opportunity for advancement to cooks and stewards." These grades enabled them to earn the same pay as petty officers though they could not exercise authority outside their branch. "Experience of many years in the Navy," the General Board

NH 89471

Legendary Sailor John Henry "Dick" Turpin was one of the Navy's first African American chief petty officers. Turpin, a crewman of the USS Maine, *survived the explosion that destroyed that warship in Havana Harbor, Cuba, in 1898. During the next decade he served in the boiler rooms and gun turrets of Navy gunboats and cruisers. Recognizing his abilities as a Sailor and a leader, in June 1917 the Navy promoted him to chief gunner's mate. After transferring to the Fleet Reserve in March 1919, Turpin worked at the Puget Sound Navy Yard, Bremerton, Washington, as a master diver. The Navy then sent the dynamic Sailor on recruitment drives around the United States. On 5 October 1925, Chief Gunner's Mate Turpin retired from the Navy after 29 years of dedicated service.*

The March on Washington

IN 1940, PRESIDENT Franklin D. Roosevelt decided to run for an unprecedented third term as the United States rearmed to meet a growing threat from the Axis Powers—Germany, Italy, and Japan. A. Philip Randolph and other African American leaders believed that the national emergency and the presidential election afforded them a unique opportunity to attack racial injustice. If African Americans, who formed an important part of the electorate in some large northern cities, rallied behind Roosevelt and his program of national defense, a grateful administration might improve the treatment of blacks. Opportunities might also open up for blacks in the armed services and the burgeoning defense industries. To dramatize African American voting power, Randolph and his colleagues planned for an enormous march on Washington, the nation's capital.

The mere threat of the march, which never took place, produced results. The President established a Fair Employment Practices Committee to persuade defense industries to make more jobs available to blacks, though it could not compel them to do so. The administration also appointed an African American, Judge William H. Hastie, as a special adviser to the Secretary of War, and promoted a black Army officer, Colonel Benjamin O. Davis Sr., to the grade of brigadier general. The government also assigned an African American reserve officer, Colonel Campbell C. Johnson, to help administer the Selective Service System, which was required by law to operate without regard to race. The Roosevelt administration's reforms, although modest at best, helped improve the lot of African Americans in defense industries and in the armed forces. Roosevelt earned the support and affection of African Americans, not only in the election of 1940, but thereafter.

Franklin D. Roosevelt greets a chief petty officer during the President's tour of the U.S. Naval Hospital in Bremerton, Washington, during World War II. The Roosevelts, especially First Lady Eleanor Roosevelt, advocated improvements in the status of black men and women in the armed forces, but not until the postwar period and the presidency of Harry S. Truman was such change institutionalized.

NH46882

observed, "has shown clearly that men of the colored race, if enlisted in any other branch than the messman's branch, and promoted to the position of petty officer, cannot maintain discipline among men of the white race over whom they may be placed by reason of their rating."

The threat of an African American march on Washington and the implied promise of the black community's support for President Franklin D. Roosevelt and his policies had a positive effect. Several prominent black leaders were appointed to positions of authority. The War Department also promised broader opportunities, including pilot training in the Army Air Corps, for black servicemen.

The Navy clung to its existing policy of segregation and restricted service, however. A panel with representatives from the Navy and Marine Corps met in July 1941 to review racial policy. At year's end it submitted two contradictory reports. The majority, consisting of all the uniformed panel members, endorsed segregation in its current form as the best means of preventing racial friction and thus ensuring efficiency. The minority report submitted by Addison Walker, a civilian special assistant to Secretary Knox, recommended assigning a small number of blacks on a few ships to duties other than those of messmen.

World War II Experience

NOT EVEN THE Japanese attack on Pearl Harbor could persuade the Navy to modify its racial policy and thus promote the more efficient use of manpower. Highlighting the absurdity of this policy, a black mess attendant, Doris Miller, helped carry the mortally wounded captain of the battleship *West Virginia* (BB 48) to cover, manned a machine gun, and earned the Navy Cross for heroism. Even after Germany and

Doris Miller, now a petty officer first class, visits the Naval Training Center at Great Lakes, Illinois, in January 1943. To boost the wartime morale of African Americans and to inspire enlistments, the Navy dispatched Miller on nationwide tours. The brave Sailor, shown wearing his Navy Cross, frequently spoke to black recruits at training stations. But Miller then returned to sea duty, and later that year made the ultimate sacrifice for his country when a Japanese submarine torpedoed and sank his ship, the escort carrier Liscome Bay *(CVE 56).*

Admiral Chester W. Nimitz, Commander in Chief of the U.S. Pacific Fleet, reads the citation awarding the Navy Cross, the service's second-highest medal, to Petty Officer Second Class Doris "Dory" Miller for his heroic actions on board battleship West Virginia *(BB 48) during the 7 December 1941 Japanese attack on Pearl Harbor.*

Italy joined forces with Japan, Secretary Knox continued to resist subtle pressure from the White House to change racial policy. He either ignored the President's wishes or responded with predictions of disaster if the status quo were changed. Those who advocated greater rights for blacks, including First Lady Eleanor Roosevelt, did not accept the secretary's arguments. In March 1942, President Roosevelt lost patience with Knox and told him that the Navy would have to accept black recruits in a proportion acceptable to the White House.

The Navy had no choice but to begin accepting black volunteers. But the number was limited to 277 each month, since only a few segregated training facilities existed. Similarly, the Marine Corps planned to train a separate defense battalion to absorb most of the 1,000 African American volunteers it was being forced to accept; the remainder would serve in a steward branch modeled after the Navy's.

The Navy might well have maintained racial segregation by enlisting only as many African Americans as could be employed as messmen or assigned to separate, largely self-contained organizations like the new Naval Construction Battalions (Seabees). Global war, however, demanded the most efficient use of manpower. Roosevelt sought to ensure this efficiency when, in December 1942, he decreed that the War Manpower Commission, not the military, would decide how

As a landing craft noses into the beach, Seabees clamor ashore during assault training. Even though construction was the primary mission of the Naval Mobile Construction Battalions (NMCBs), they also prepared for combat. The Navy employed several mostly black Seabee units.

NA 208-N-5704

NA 80-G-21743

Not content to remain in the galley below decks during combat in the Pacific, the African American Sailors in this photo volunteered to man antiaircraft guns on board heavy cruiser Indianapolis (CA 35). *Many* Indianapolis *crewmen died when a Japanese submarine sank the ship in July 1945.*

18

African Americans in the U.S. Coast Guard

THROUGHOUT the existence of the U.S. Coast Guard, an amalgam of the Revenue Cutter Service, Life Saving Service, and Light House Service, black Americans served with distinction, although often in segregated contingents. African Americans manned life-saving stations, tended lighthouses, and served in the Coast Guard messman's branch.

In January 1942, the Commandant of the U.S. Coast Guard, Rear Admiral Russell R. Waesche, enlisted 500 African Americans into the service, which was under the Navy during the war.

Like millions of other American seamen, Fireman First Class Charles Tyner, a coastguardsman, went in harm's way during World War II. Enemy fire put the jagged hole in his helmet during the 1944 invasion of southern France.

The U.S. Coast Guard's first African American officers, Lieutenants (jg) Joseph C. Jenkins (left) and Clarence Samuels, brave winter weather in the North Atlantic during 1943 on board USS Sea Cloud, *a Navy-chartered ship operated by the Coast Guard. The Coast Guard commissioned the two men a full year before the Navy took similar steps. The Navy's sister seagoing service employed* Sea Cloud *to test the feasibility of fully integrating the officer and enlisted ranks of a crew; the experiment was a success.*

He assigned the black coastguardsmen to billets on small craft or in port security detachments and enabled them to compete for promotion to petty officer. The chairman of the Navy's General Board, Vice Admiral Walton R. Sexton, objected to this effort. He warned that the influx of even 500 blacks might prevent the Coast Guard from maintaining racial segregation because of its small size. Nonetheless, the first of these African American recruits entered training at Manhattan Beach, California, in the spring of 1942, the Coast Guard's first step toward integrating the races.

By war's end, 5,000 African Americans served in the Coast Guard. Although most blacks still functioned as stewards, the Coast Guard, as Admiral Sexton had predicted, could not maintain segregation; indeed, it chose not to. African American officers and petty officers exercised authority over whites on a racially integrated weather ship, an escort vessel, and some smaller craft.

Black Sailors of Camp Robert Smalls' Chemical Warfare Division demonstrate the use of gas masks during a drill at Great Lakes Naval Training Station in September 1943.

many black Americans the services would induct through the Selective Service System.

The Impact of Selective Service on the Navy

Because of Roosevelt's action, African Americans entered the Navy by the thousands instead of the hundreds. The Navy increased the number of messmen, organized more construction battalions for blacks, and established base units in which African American Sailors served as stevedores. Indeed, most of the blacks serving in 1943 functioned as laborers at ports, bases, or ammunition depots in the United States or over-

Although rates were opened to all qualified personnel by mid-1942, the Navy remained racially segregated at its training schools, even during pastime activities such as sports, drama, and band. Segregated seating for events like this 1943 concert featuring black singer and actor Paul Robeson was a common site at Great Lakes Naval Training Station.

The Navy's "Golden Thirteen." In March 1944, these men became the first African Americans to be commissioned as officers (and one warrant officer) in the U.S. Naval Reserve. This was an especially important event for the Navy and for American society. Bottom row, left to right, are Ensigns James E. Hair, Samuel E. Barnes, George C. Cooper, William S. White, and Dennis D. Nelson II; middle row, left to right, are Ensign Graham E. Martin, Warrant Officer Charles B. Lear, and Ensigns Phillip G. Barnes and Reginald E. Goodwin; top row, left to right, Ensigns John W. Reagan, Jesse W. Arbor, Dalton L. Baugh, and Frank E. Sublett Jr.

already commissioned two African Americans.

Instead, the Navy's Bureau of Naval Personnel decided to choose officer candidates from among the African American Sailors already on duty. Of the sixteen candidates who entered an accelerated program of training in January 1944, twelve became ensigns in the Naval Reserve on 17 March. The newly commissioned officers were: James E. Hair, Samuel E. Barnes, George C. Cooper, William S. White, Dennis D. Nelson II, Graham E. Martin, Phillip G. Barnes, Reginald E. Goodwin, John W. Reagan, Jesse W. Arbor, Dalton L. Baugh, and Frank E. Sublett Jr. Another of the candidates, Charles B. Lear, became a warrant officer, apparently because he lacked a college education. The group later came to be called

seas. Most African American Sailors performed duties indirectly related to combat, even the mess attendants on board warships who functioned primarily as cooks, waiters, and housekeepers. Forced into a narrow range of specialties, black Sailors saw themselves as outsiders, excluded from the real Navy, serving as workers rather than fighters.

The influx of African Americans into the Navy's enlisted ranks dramatized the absence of blacks in the officer corps. No black had ever received a commission, but in September 1943 Adlai E. Stevenson, an assistant to Secretary Knox, believed that the time had come to shatter precedent. Indeed, change had become all but inevitable. A dozen blacks—including a light-complexioned medical student, Bernard W. Robinson, apparently mistaken for a white—were already enrolled during 1943 and 1944 at various campuses in the V-12 officer-training program, the precursor of the postwar Naval Reserve Officer Training Corps. Stevenson proposed accelerating the process by commissioning "10 or 12 negroes selected from top notch civilians." To prod the Navy into action, he pointed out that the Coast Guard had

A trio of Sailors from Mason (DE 529) proudly look over their ship after her commissioning on 20 March 1944 at the Boston Navy Yard. The Navy assigned to the Mason mostly black enlisted men, but only white officers.

the "Golden Thirteen." The twelve who received commissions broke the racial barrier, creating the opening through which Jesse L. Brown would enter pilot training and the naval officer corps.

The commissioning of the Navy's first black officers became the subject of a story in *Life* magazine and an inspiration to all African Americans, but it did not break Jim Crow's grip on the Navy. The handful of white officers who had helped shepherd Stevenson's proposal through the Navy's administrative hierarchy knew that something more had to be done. These officers —Captain Thomas F. Darden and Lieutenant Commanders Charles E.

In April 1944, two years after the Navy opened its enlisted ratings to all qualified men, Aviation Machinist's Mate Third Class Alvin V. Morrison carries out maintenance on a PBY patrol plane at Naval Air Station, Seattle.

NA 80-G-233274

The predominantly black enlisted crew of submarine chaser PC 1264, *along with white officers and petty officers, put their ship in commission at ceremonies in New York City on 25 April 1944. Eventually, black officers and petty officers integrated the crews of other World War II naval vessels.*

NH 92463

Dillon, Donald G. Van Ness, and Christopher Sargent—formed the Navy Department's Special Programs Unit. The Special Programs Unit arranged for a leadership course at Great Lakes designed to prepare graduates for promotion to petty officer. To take advantage of the new course, the Bureau of Naval Personnel went so far as to permit the promotion of qualified blacks to petty officer even though specific openings for them did not yet exist.

Because Secretary Knox still favored separating the races, African American Sailors would have to serve on specific ships under the command of white officers and petty officers. As a result, the Chief of Naval Operations, Admiral Ernest J. King, in January 1944 ordered the assignment of 196 black Sailors and forty-four white officers and petty officers to the destroyer escort *Mason* and fifty-three black seamen and fourteen white officers and petty officers to the submarine

The Port Chicago disaster. On 17 July 1944, an enormous explosion at the Naval Magazine in Port Chicago, California, destroyed two ships and nearby buildings. The blast also killed 320 Sailors, two-thirds of them African Americans who had been loading ammunition onto cargo ships. Angry that predominantly black units were tasked with the dangerous duty of handling ammunition, the survivors refused to work. A number of these men were sentenced to prison or given dishonorable discharges.

chaser *PC 1264*. Another four submarine chasers later joined in the experiment. Gradually, black petty officers replaced their white counterparts and some black officers were assigned as they became available.

Concerns surfaced almost immediately that African American Sailors would not respect petty officers of their own race and that the petty officers would prove reluctant to discipline their fellow blacks. These fears never became reality, however. The Navy's *Guide to Command of Negro Naval Personnel*, published in 1945 and apparently intended mainly for white officers, declared: "Contrary to a fairly gen-

eral belief, it has been found that Negro Naval personnel respond readily to good Negro leadership." Moreover, the guide continued, "Experience has taught . . . that colored personnel can be directed and disciplined with less likelihood of dissatisfaction by Negro than by white officers, provided the former are well selected and competent." Left unsaid was the fact that careful selection and competence were equally important for white officers in command of whites.

When Secretary Knox died suddenly on 28 April 1944, the President replaced him with Under Secretary of the Navy James V.

Forrestal, a prewar investment banker who had been active in the National Urban League, a civil rights organization. The barriers separating the races had already been lowered to permit African Americans to become officers and petty officers and to serve at sea in a variety of specialties other than steward. The new Secretary of the Navy, however, faced a racially based crisis in morale. African Americans resented the narrow range of opportunity open to most of them, and white seamen objected to the prospect of repeated tours of sea duty and the likelihood of combat because black Sailors filled many shore-based billets.

Lester B. Granger, a prominent figure in the African American community, inspects the working conditions of black Sailors at Naval Air Station, San Diego, in June 1945. To oversee racial matters in the Navy, President Roosevelt had appointed Granger to the staff of Secretary of the Navy James Forrestal. After the war, Granger led the National Urban League.

An obvious solution would have been to assign trained African Americans throughout the fleet, but Forrestal knew that the bureaucracy had torpedoed such a broad proposal earlier. On 20 May 1944, the Secretary of the Navy therefore proposed the assignment of qualified blacks to large auxiliaries—oilers, ammunition ships, and transports—rather than to combat ships. In no case would African Americans exceed 10 percent of the total crew. Forrestal was making a concession to Rear Admiral Randall Jacobs, Chief of the Bureau of Naval Personnel, who remained convinced that "you couldn't dump 200 colored boys on a crew in battle."

President Roosevelt approved the idea. Admiral King set the measure in motion and Admiral Jacobs carried it out. What began as an experiment soon became policy, as the Navy routinely assigned African Americans to a lengthening list of fleet auxiliaries and ultimately to all such ships.

This measure coincided with an effort to desegregate support units after a tragic explosion of two ammunition ships being loaded at Port Chicago, California. The blast, on 17 July 1944, killed 320 Sailors, 202 of them members of an African American labor unit. When 50 of the badly shaken survivors, all of them African American, refused to return to the dangerous work, the Navy tried them for mutiny. Those believed to be the ringleaders were sentenced to prison, while most of the others received bad-conduct discharges. The Navy, in reaction to the public outcry over the affair, reduced the proportion of blacks in ammunition handling units. After the war, the service took into account the impact of the deaths and destruction on those who survived and reduced their punishments.

Segregation survived in the new logistic support companies that replaced depot companies at advance bases overseas. There was at least one exception, however. When a segregated unit, totaling some 400 black Sailors, arrived at a Pacific advance base in the spring of 1944, Commander W. Biddle Combs, the commanding officer, decided on his own initiative that the races should serve side by side. His innovation did not cause serious morale problems and raised efficiency.

Secretary Forrestal continued to advocate equal treatment and greater opportunity for black Sailors. In March 1945, he appointed an African American, Lester B. Granger, as his civilian aide to monitor implementation of the Navy's racial policy. Thanks to their efforts, by the end of the war, the Navy counted 164,942 African American Sailors (including about 60 enlisted women), 5.37 percent of the total enlisted strength. Although more than twice the prewar percentage, this was roughly half the proportion of blacks in the overall population. Moreover, some 40 percent of the African American enlisted men served in the Steward Branch. No one could predict how many of these men and the sixty black officers, all of the latter reservists on active duty, would survive the demobilization of the wartime Navy and continue to serve in the smaller peacetime establishment.

Into the Cold War

AS WORLD WAR II drew to a close, Secretary Forrestal pursued the objective of providing equal treatment and opportunity for all races while causing a minimum of commotion in the ranks. A committee headed by Captain Roscoe H. Hillenkoetter conducted a study that examined existing policy and the changes proposed by Lester Granger, Forrestal's adviser on racial matters. After endorsing the conclusion that racial segregation resulted in inefficient use of manpower, the group called for a policy that would promote efficiency by assigning every Sailor according to his ability and the needs of the service, rather than on the basis of race.

Granger made an inspection tour in August 1945 that reinforced his belief that efficiency improved as a result of racial integration. Morale, he reported, tended to be low in those labor units manned mostly by African Americans. Granger was especially concerned that the Steward Branch, with its dominant African American representation, could well disrupt the integration process.

In the postwar Navy, African Americans were to be eligible for "all types of assignments in all ratings in all activities and all ships of the naval service." By 1 October 1946, African American Sailors, with the exception of the stewards at the Naval Academy, were reassigned so the proportion of blacks in any ship or activity would not exceed 10 percent.

After the war, a recently commissioned Navy officer, Charles F. Rauch Jr., reported to the cruiser *Huntington* (CL 107) and discovered that the Navy was indeed integrating the enlisted ranks. The crew included black petty officers whose duties had nothing to do with preparing or serving food. Although the stewards, whether African American or Filipino, formed a distinct servant class, the young officer considered

Lieutenant (jg) Harriet Ida Pickens and Ensign Frances Eliza Wills, the first African American WAVES commissioned in the U.S. Navy, prepare to travel to their duty assignment at the Hunter Naval Training Station in New York. The women had graduated from the Naval Reserve Midshipman's School at Smith College in Northampton, Massachusetts.

NA 80-G-48365

the black seamen simply as members of the crew. He did not realize that black Sailors were encountering resistance to integration by some of their shipmates.

Despite Secretary Forrestal's intentions, African Americans continued to be clustered in the Steward Branch, with only a few men serving in other billets, a result of racial segregation in the schools.

As the Navy drastically contracted in size after the war, it raised enlistment standards. Since blacks were more likely than whites to have graduated from substandard schools, African American recruits tended to make lower scores on general qualification tests. Thus, many black Sailors were unable to qualify for non-steward billets. As

late as 1948, of all the African Americans in the Navy (including about 20 enlisted women), 62 percent served as stewards.

During the war, two African American women, Harriet Pickens and Frances Wills, were commissioned in the WAVES (Women Accepted for Volunteer Service), the Navy's wartime auxiliary for women. Although the WAVES became a part of the Navy, both officers returned to civilian life after the war. Four African American women—Edith Devoe, Phyllis Mae Dailey, Maxine Magee, and Eula Stimley—held reserve commissions in the Navy Nurse Corps. By 1951, however, only two black nurses served on active duty, Lieutenant (jg) Ellen Stricklin and DeVoe, also

a lieutenant (jg), who had earned a regular commission.

The number of male African American officers declined dramatically after the war. From a wartime peak of sixty, the total dwindled by the end of 1946 to just three, all of them reservists on extended active duty. As Forrestal's successor Secretary of the Navy John L. Sullivan later explained, the service had slipped back into its comfortable prewar ways, with enlisted blacks waiting on white officers.

Not until 1947 did Ensign John Lee, commissioned in the reserves from the V-12 program during the war, become the first African American officer in the regular Navy. As Lee described it, his selection for a regular commission

On 8 March 1948, Commander Thomas Gaylord swears in five newly commissioned Navy nurses, including Phyllis Mae Daily, the first African American to join the ranks of the Navy Nurse Corps.

NA 80-G-48365

Ensign John Wesley Lee, USN, a product of the wartime V-12 training program, was the first African American to earn a commission in the regular Navy. Training at the General Line School in Newport and sea duty on board the carrier Kearsarge *(CV 33) qualified Lee for his commission when the service was actively recruiting black officers for the regular Navy.*

resulted from being in the right place at the right time. In 1947, when the only African American midshipman at the Naval Academy, Wesley A. Brown, was two years away from graduation, the Navy became disturbed by the lack of even one African American regular officer. Moreover, almost all of the black reserve officers commissioned during the war had left the service. One of the three men on active duty during the previous year, Lieutenant (jg) Samuel L. Gravely, had just left, since he was convinced that opportunities for an African American officer were severely limited. The remaining two reservists available for a place in the regular Navy were Lieutenant (jg) Dennis D. Nelson and Lee. The Bureau of Naval Personnel considered Nelson too old at age forty to receive a regular commission, but Lee was in his mid-twenties. Lee realized that he

needed further training and duty at sea to complete a successful career in the Navy. Captain Roland N. Smoot, Director of Officer Personnel, agreed with Lee and sent him to the General Line School at Newport, Rhode Island, followed by an assignment to the aircraft carrier *Kearsarge* (CV 33).

Various obstacles hampered efforts to increase the number of black officers. Those commissioned in the reserves during World War II tended to be older than the typical newly commissioned ensign of that time. Hence, they were older than most officers in the same pay grade, and the Navy emphasized retention of younger officers. Moreover, the Navy's officer candidate program—which had produced the Golden Thirteen—contracted after the war. The Naval Reserve Officer Training Corps (NROTC) at various colleges and universities became the normal

source for reserve officers. Between 1946 and 1948, only sixteen blacks completed officer candidate school, and only fourteen African Americans (contrasted with 5,600 whites) graduated from NROTC programs.

Compounding the problem, the Navy excluded traditionally black schools like Howard University in Washington, D.C., from the wartime V-12 officer training program, and that ban continued to apply to the postwar NROTC. Every college or university that participated in officer training agreed to accept anyone who had earned an NROTC scholarship in a competitive examination, but some ignored the pledge because of state law, local tradition, or school policy. As a result, African Americans who qualified for the program had to find an institution that would accept them. For example, Jesse Brown enrolled at Ohio State University and joined the NROTC program before leaving the school to enter pilot training.

A simple solution would have been to include black institutions in the list of schools offering NROTC training, but this option aroused scant enthusiasm, even among some Americans who favored racial integration. They feared that the black schools would attract too many African American midshipmen and thus reinforce racial segregation in higher education at a time when barriers separating the races were beginning to come down. Not until 1965 did the Navy establish an NROTC unit at a traditionally black college— Prairie View A&M in Texas.

Although the Navy's racial policy had turned away from segregation toward integration, practice did not yet conform to policy. Numbers

Lieutenant (jg) Dennis D. Nelson, USNR. Commissioned in the Naval Reserve during World War II and a member of the Golden Thirteen, Nelson was one of only three African American naval officers, all reservists, still on active duty at the end of 1946. Nelson became the Navy's strongest advocate for personnel reform at the time, serving as an adviser on recruitment to the Secretary of the Navy and the Fahy Committee and setting up a special program to attract blacks to the naval service. Nelson eventually received a regular commission and retired from the Navy as a lieutenant commander.

alone demonstrated that neither the existing officer corps, nor the NROTC, nor the Naval Academy, which had only five African American midshipmen in 1949, could claim meaningful integration. Similarly, the enlisted force was only 4.3 percent black in 1948. The trifling number of officers, and the continued existence of a predominately black Steward Branch, raised questions, especially in the African American press, about the Navy's actual commitment to equal treatment and opportunity.

Few outside observers knew, however, that the Bureau of Naval Personnel did attempt to correct those instances of racial discrimination that came to its attention. These largely unpublicized corrective actions dealt with specific incidents and did not alter the impression among African Americans that the Navy's commitment to racial

integration had little substance. During his efforts to persuade blacks to take the examination for NROTC scholarships, Lieutenant Nelson learned of the depth of black disenchantment with the Navy. He and his special recruiting team addressed some 17,000 black high-school students in 1948 and 1949 but persuaded only ninety men to compete.

President Truman Acts

The Cold War that pitted the United States against the USSR grew dangerously warm in 1948 when the Soviet Union blocked access to Berlin in occupied Germany and took other hostile actions around the world. In this global confrontation, the United States could not afford to squander its resources, including manpower. Specifically, the nation could no longer relegate African Americans to

nonessential tasks, in effect ignoring the potential skills of one citizen in ten, merely to maintain racial segregation. Not only did segregation waste manpower, it tarnished the image of the United States as the champion of the free world and offended African nations with resources that included oil and uranium.

Harry S. Truman, who had succeeded to the presidency in April 1945 when Franklin Roosevelt died, needed political support in the election of 1948 from African Americans and those in the Democratic Party who favored racial tolerance. Politics thus influenced Truman, even though he strongly opposed racism, when on 26 July 1948 he issued Executive Order 9981, which established a policy of "equality of treatment and opportunity for all persons in the armed services without regard to race, color, religion, or national origin." The President took the announced policy seriously, for the executive order also set up a committee to examine the response to the directive and to make appropriate recommendations to the commander in chief. When asked during a press conference if the executive order meant "eventually the end of segregation," Truman answered with one word, "Yes."

Captain Herbert D. Riley, a naval officer on the staff of James Forrestal, now Secretary of Defense, warned that resistance to the racial integration of officers' clubs and wardrooms might result in mass resignations and early retirements. Riley even raised the specter of mutiny, but his fears did not reflect the views of the Navy as an institution. Policies designed to broaden

President Truman's Executive Order 9981

DESPITE GROWING UP in racially segregated Missouri, Truman revealed, while still a senator, a belief that African Americans should enjoy the basic rights guaranteed to all citizens. A wave of violence against blacks that swept the country after World War II strengthened the President's resolve. He seemed especially angered by an assault of South Carolina lawmen on Isaac Woodard, an Army veteran honorably discharged and still wearing his uniform as he returned home. After an unprovoked beating, the injured man was thrown in jail, where he suffered for hours without medical attention. When he was released, only an Army hospital would treat the injuries that left him blind.

Such brutality toward African Americans and the denial of their basic rights angered Truman. His commitment to the welfare of blacks did not include complete social equality, however, for he had not shaken off all the customs of his native state. Truman nonetheless pressed for an end to officially sanctioned segregation. In 1947 he convened a President's Committee on Civil rights that recommended, among other things, the racial integration of the armed forces.

Truman's reaction to injustice helped prod him into action, but he also had political motives. Clark Clifford and other advisers warned him that the Republican Party could tip the balance against him in the 1948 presidential election by introducing legislation sought by African Americans—anti-lynching or fair employment practices bills, for instance. If these bills passed, or segregationist Democrats succeeded in torpedoing the Republican initiatives, blacks in

President Harry S. Truman

the large northern cities might well desert the President. Something had to be done to ensure African American loyalty, especially since the likely Republican nominee, former Governor Thomas E. Dewey of New York, had been a strong advocate of civil rights.

At first, Truman's political instincts failed him. He did not heed Clifford's advice to bring blacks into a coalition with two groups the Republicans had alienated—farmers and organized labor. Even though the President moved warily, compromise proved impossible. The segregationist Democrats bolted from the convention and formed a new party, the Dixiecrats, who nominated a candidate of their own. When Truman issued Executive Order 9981 on 26 July 1948, the coalition envisioned by Clifford rapidly took shape. The votes of urban blacks, along with the support of blue-collar workers and farmers, enabled Truman to win a narrow victory in November 1948.

opportunities for blacks already existed. Assistant Secretary of the Navy (Air) John Nicholas Brown advised Forrestal in December 1948 that, as a result of these policies, most white officers and enlisted men had come to accept the principle of equal treatment and opportunity regardless of race. Moreover African Americans served in a variety of duties on board ship and ashore where they berthed and worked alongside whites.

Nevertheless, problems remained, especially with the continuing heavy concentration of blacks in the Steward Branch. By suspending the recruiting of African Americans to the Steward Branch, the Bureau of Naval Personnel hoped to improve the balance of blacks and non-blacks in the branch. After World War II, the Navy actively recruited Chamorros from Guam and Filipinos. Even so, two out of three stewards were black.

The Review of Truman's New Racial Policy

President Truman wasted no time in appointing the review committee called for in Executive Order 9981. In September 1948, he announced the formation of a panel headed by Charles P. Fahy, an attorney and former Solicitor General of the United States. The President and his advisers concluded that a committee dealing with so sensitive an issue as race relations had to have a white chairman. Truman insisted on someone who was sympathetic to the aspirations of blacks and could express his views in a way that did not grate on the ears of white Southerners. Fahy, a native of Georgia with a liberal attitude on questions of race, fit that descrip-

President Harry S. Truman with Secretary of Defense James V. Forrestal to his right, poses with the Fahy Committee, which he appointed in September 1948 to review race relations and the progress made by the armed services in integrating the forces. The committee's report noted the dearth of African Americans in the naval service and the tendency of the Navy to concentrate blacks in the Steward Branch. As a result of committee recommendations, the Navy intensified its recruitment of African Americans for both the general service and NROTC scholarship programs. The naval service also dropped the demand for higher test scores from black recruits and made chief stewards chief petty officers.

tion. The Fahy Committee—consisting of five whites and two African Americans—met for the first time in January 1949 to review the progress toward integration made by the armed forces.

After reviewing the Navy's program for providing equal treatment and opportunity to African Americans, the Fahy Committee asked why so few served in the Navy, and why so many of those who did were stewards. The Chief of Naval Personnel, Vice Admiral William Fechteler replied that blacks were not a seafaring people. Fechteler thought he had answered both questions, but his explanation did not satisfy the committee, nor did the information that there were a number of African Americans training at Naval Reserve facilities and that

Jesse Brown was undergoing carrier qualification.

During the committee's sessions, Lieutenant Nelson and other Navy representatives revealed that there were no programs to recruit or commission blacks. As a result, the Navy tasked Nelson with setting up such a special program. To carry it out, he chose five African American reserve officers, all but one of whom had been commissioned during World War II.

Lieutenant Nelson's success in attracting blacks to the naval service as officers or enlisted men, and the process of advising the Secretary of the Navy, had mixed effects on his Navy career. These activities kept him anchored to a desk, depriving him of the seagoing experience that counted heavily toward promotion or integration into the regular Navy.

According to a fellow black officer, Samuel Gravely, Nelson made that choice regardless of cost to himself, because he felt it vital to the future of black Americans in the Navy.

Gravely described Nelson as the sort of man "who did not hesitate to state his opinions and seek the support of the Secretary of the Navy," traits that did not endear him to his uniformed superiors. Nevertheless, Nelson received a regular commission and retired as a lieutenant commander, largely because of his valuable work for the secretary in connection with the Fahy Committee and its reforms.

After being recalled to active duty as a member of Nelson's group, Lieutenant (jg) John W. Reagan discovered that fellow African Americans were skeptical of his recruiting pitch. Some potential

Ensign Wesley A. Brown and his mother Rosetta at his graduation from the U.S. Naval Academy in 1949. Brown overcame institutional and social prejudice to become the first African American to complete the rigorous, four-year program at Annapolis. He entered the Civil Engineering Corps, rose to the rank of lieutenant commander, and finished a successful career in the Navy before retiring in 1969.

candidates for NROTC, despite Reagan's own example, doubted that a black man in the Navy could become more than an enlisted steward.

In the spring of 1949, as the Fahy Committee continued its deliberations, Ensign Wesley Brown became the first African American to graduate from the U.S. Naval Academy. A native of Washington,

D.C., Brown had received his appointment thanks to Representative Adam Clayton Powell Jr., an African American whose congressional district in New York included the black enclave of Harlem.

Other African Americans, including George Trivers, who entered the Academy in 1937, had failed to graduate. Overwhelmed by hazing and forced isolation, they

chose to earn a degree elsewhere. Brown, especially after he spoke with Trivers, feared the worst, but his experience at Annapolis proved less stressful than he expected. Most of Brown's fellow midshipmen, unlike many of Trivers' hostile classmates of the 1930s, for the most part just ignored him. A few men were openly friendly and two or three even offered to room with him. Brown chose to live alone, however, for he was concerned that a white roommate might face some form of retaliation. During his time at the Academy, Brown discovered that not every Northerner was liberal on racial matters, nor every Southerner a bigot.

Representative Powell, who frequently questioned the Navy's commitment to equal treatment and opportunity, insisted from the outset that Brown receive fair treatment. When Powell complained to Secretary Forrestal of a plot to grade Brown more strictly than white midshipmen, the Secretary of the Navy forwarded the complaint to Vice Admiral Aubrey W. Fitch, Superintendent of the Naval Academy. Confident that Powell had invented the issue to pressure the Navy toward racial integration, Fitch questioned the midshipman. Brown's surprised reaction not only validated Fitch's belief but also revealed that the midshipman was not a party to the congressman's plan. The graduation of Wesley Brown in 1949 broke the racial barrier at the Naval Academy, but not until 1953 did a second African American, Lawrence Chambers, receive a commission.

In the summer of 1949, the Fahy Committee proposed its solution to the Navy's racial problems. First, the service should launch a vigorous campaign to recruit blacks for both the general service and the NROTC. To take the curse off the Steward Branch, the Navy should treat chief stewards like chief petty officers in all other specialties. In addition, the Navy should settle for the same mental standards required of recruits by the other services, in-

stead of demanding higher test scores.

Senior officers of the Bureau of Naval Personnel objected to making the chief steward a peer of the chief petty officer and warned that uniform test scores for all the services would mean lower scores for enlistment in the Navy. Under

---

"Negroes who are in the schools are there because they meet the qualifications of a particular rating. And meeting these qualifications, they elicit the respect which craftsmanship deserves."

—Fahy Committee

Secretary of the Navy Dan A. Kimball, however, accepted the spirit if not the letter of the committee's recommendations. He intensified the recruiting of African Americans, pledged that the Marine Corps would integrate recruit training as the Navy had done since 1945, agreed to enhance the status of chief stewards, and promised to undertake a study of possible assignments for recruits with lower test scores. The commit-

tee endorsed Kimball's plan, which Secretary of Defense Louis D. Johnson, who had replaced Forrestal in March, formally announced on 7 June 1949.

In August 1949, representatives of the Fahy Committee traveled to the Great Lakes Naval Training Station near Chicago. There they also visited the technical training schools, which provided instruction in electronics, communications, and other demanding subjects. The group reported that Great Lakes was "unquestionably following the policy of the Navy." The visit revealed "no segregation in either boot training or in the service schools." Clearly, "Negroes who are in the schools are there because they meet the qualifications of a particular rating. And meeting these qualifications, they elicit the respect which craftsmanship deserves."

Challenges To Be Met

Although the Fahy Committee ratified the Navy's efforts to achieve equal treatment and opportunity for all races, problems remained. The question of social integration had to be resolved. Lieutenant Nelson believed that "personal relationships" in the Navy's enlisted force "were developing normally with a minimum of obstructions." When these obstructions arose, such as racial segregation at barber shops or swimming pools, the Navy invoked a directive of 23 June 1949, which sought to achieve the goal of President Truman's policy by, among other things, prohibiting "special or unusual provisions"—in these instances racial segregation— in housing, messing, berthing or

Representative Adam Clayton Powell Jr. (D-New York), who had appointed Wesley Brown to the U.S. Naval Academy, continued to press the Navy to lessen the number of blacks in the Steward Branch.

those invited to join cruises meant to impress influential civilians with the importance of the Navy. In 1949, representatives of the black press went on board the battleship *Missouri* (BB 63) for a cruise to European ports. One of the African American reporters, Lucius Harper of the *Chicago Defender*, discovered during the cruise that some of the 104 black crewmen serving in the ship either were operating or learning to operate radar, manning gun turrets, or performing mechanical or engineering duties. He conceded that racial integration was not "perfect or fool-proof"—as the existence of the Steward Branch made up exclusively of blacks testified—but he believed that the stewards could be integrated racially through examinations and promotions. Nelson interpreted Harper's article as evidence that the *Chicago Defender* and similar newspapers would continue to criticize actual instances of racial discrimination but "go more than half way in promoting and encouraging the aims of the integrated United States Navy."

Despite the signs of generally harmonious race relations within the Navy, misunderstandings sometimes arose with civilians when the Navy insisted on the racial integration of community-sponsored events for its officers and enlisted men. At Charleston, South Carolina, in the spring of 1950, the captain of the aircraft carrier *Saipan* (CVL 48) cooperated with the whites-only YMCA to hold a party on board the ship. Black crewmembers were not specifically excluded, and some did attend. The following night, the white YMCA and its black counterpart staged a separate party, exclusively for the African

other facilities "for the accommodation of any minority race."

Problems surfaced most readily in the southern United States, where a naval or military installation formed a racially integrated island in a sea of segregation. Despite local law as well as custom, by mid-1950 the Navy had integrated recreational and other facilities at bases in Jacksonville and Pensacola, Florida, and Corpus Christi, Texas.

Lieutenant Nelson enlisted the black press on behalf of the Navy's efforts to integrate the races. He also convinced his superiors to include African American journalists among

33

During the summer cruises of 1949 and 1950, African American journalists sailed on board battleship **Missouri** *(BB 63) to report on the Navy's progress with integrating crews. The reporters concluded that the Navy was committed to equal treatment but that racial discrimination still existed.*

American crewmen, in the racially segregated city. The captain of *Saipan* played no part in planning the second party but accepted on behalf of his crew the invitation extended by the sponsors.

Learning of the racially segregated parties, which caught the eye of the *Chicago Defender*, Secretary of the Navy Francis P. Matthews, who had been in office since the summer of 1949, ordered an investigation. Based on this review he decided that *Saipan*'s skipper "did not knowingly sanction a segregated program," but he warned all commanding officers to avoid segregated events like those at Charleston. Matthews also advised the Chicago newspaper, that the Navy would not officially endorse, sanction, promote, or subsidize such activity.

The Navy's racial policy underwent another test at an unlikely place, the city of Halifax in the

Canadian province of Nova Scotia. *Missouri*, with black journalists again on board for a cruise, tied up there during the summer of 1950. The battleship's officers accepted assurances by a liaison officer from the Royal Canadian Navy that no color line existed at Halifax. When the local Colored Citizens Improvement League invited the ship's black Sailors to a party, *Missouri*'s captain assumed that this event would take place in addition to a similar event for the entire crew and promptly accepted on behalf of the African American crewmembers. Unfortunately, the captain was mistaken. In spite of the liaison officer's statement, racial segregation prevailed in Nova Scotia as it did in South Carolina. The sponsors at Halifax were planning two separate parties, one for whites and the other for blacks.

Once again, Secretary Matthews ordered an investigation. After

weighing the evidence, he concluded that "the *Missouri* has enjoyed an excellent record in its efforts to achieve full integration and I am certain segregation of crew members at Halifax by special invitations was not intended or implied." He warned, however, that incidents like that at Halifax must not recur.

Lester Granger, formerly an aide to Secretary of the Navy Forrestal and now the executive director of the National Urban League, underscored the Navy's determination to put an end to segregated social and recreational events. He contacted B. A. Husbands, president of the Halifax Colored Citizens Improvement League, and pointed out that the Navy could not "insist upon the elimination of racial separation aboard ship and in any other service activities, and at the same time accept invitations which are restricted to Negro servicemen."

Secretary of the Navy Francis P. Matthews, a long-time proponent of black advancement in the naval service, speaks to a **Philippine Sea** *(CV 47) crewman during Matthews' visit to the fleet off Korea in November 1950.*

When war broke out in Korea during June 1950, Secretary of the Navy Matthews—a member of the President's Committee on Civil Rights—was systematically carrying out the reforms that Under Secretary Kimball had adopted to satisfy the Fahy Committee. Matthews in July 1949 issued an order banning discrimination on the basis of race, color, religion, or national origin in the enlistment, appointment, promotion, or assignment of Navy or Marine Corps personnel. He thus strengthened a policy of equal treatment and opportunity adopted in 1945 and reaffirmed in 1946.

Matthews then turned to the specific assurances given the committee by Under Secretary Kimball. On 25 July 1949, chief stewards became chief petty officers. Stewards first, second, and third class, however, remained in organizational limbo. Not until the end of August did the Bureau of Naval Personnel approve a recommendation from Lieutenant Nelson, now an officer of the regular Navy, to designate the lower ranking stewards as petty officers in their appropriate grades.

A general perception that stewards were not real Sailors delayed the full acceptance of senior stewards as genuine petty officers. In the autumn of 1950, for instance, *All Hands: The Bureau of Naval Personnel Information Bulletin* printed a patronizing account of the work of some stewards at the Naval Air Station, Atlantic City, New Jersey. In their off-duty time they had planted and tended a garden which yielded a crop of vegetables that would have cost the Navy at least $1,000 to purchase from local farms. This accomplishment, however, remained buried amid the cuteness of a story that began: "Now that the frost is on the pumpkin and ruin reigns for the potato patch, the wardroom folks . . . sometimes sit back and reflect on the success of their 1950 garden plot." Although the headline referred to the stewards as "Men of the Sea," a reader could not help but conclude that they preferred "the memory of roasting ears and fresh green cucumbers" to the perils of the deep.

Impact of the Korean War

THE NAVY PERSISTED during the Korean War in its efforts to attract African Americans. The service dispatched recruiters to speak to black high school students. After a decline from 17,518 in 1949 to 14,842 in 1950, the number of African American Sailors reached 17,598 in 1951 and surpassed 24,000 by the end of the fighting in July 1953. The number of blacks in the enlisted force had increased by 7,000 after establishment of the Fahy Committee in 1949. Equally encouraging was the fact that some 2,700 blacks applied during 1949 to enter NROTC, either by competing for scholarships or joining units at colleges where they already were enrolled.

When African American officers, many serving as recruiters, were ordered to sea, they tended to be assigned as assistant communications officers on board ships. Indeed, over the years black officers were often first assigned to recruiting duty for one or two tours and then to an auxiliary vessel like an oiler, where they might well take charge of the radio shack. Assignments like these did not enhance an officer's

chances for promotion. Not until the late 1950s did naval personnel officers, called detailers, make a conscientious effort to place officers, regardless of race, where their abilities best fulfilled the Navy's needs.

One of the officers brought back by Nelson specifically for recruiting duty followed the common assign-

ment pattern of young black officers. Lieutenant Gravely proceeded from recruiting duty to communications school and then to an assistant communications billet, on board a naval vessel, in his case the battleship *Iowa (BB 61)*. He served in the mighty warship when she shelled targets in North Korea. He assumed that he had been selected

*Battleship **Iowa** (BB 61) fires a 16-inch shell at a target in North Korea. Brought back into active service for the Korean War, **Iowa** served as the Seventh Fleet flagship during her April to October 1952 combat deployment.*

Rear Admiral Samuel L. Gravely Jr. accepts the congratulations of fellow officers in June 1971 on his promotion to flag rank, the first African American thus honored. Gravely was commissioned through the Navy's World War II V-12 program. During the Korean War he served on board the battleship Iowa *(BB 61). In 1976, Gravely was promoted to vice admiral and assigned command of the Third Fleet.*

for communications duty because he had been the communications officer in the submarine chaser *PC 1264* during World War II. But, he soon realized that "the Navy really didn't pick its best people" for this assignment. Gravely, however, was determined to succeed in the Navy. He earned a regular commission, and fashioned a successful career path in surface warfare, taking command of destroyer escort *Falgout* (DE 324) in 1961. On 28 April 1971, in recognition of Gravely's superior leadership skills, the Navy selected him for flag rank—the first African American to become an admiral.

Lieutenant Lee, the first African American commissioned in the regular Navy, served in the cruiser *Toledo* (CL 133) during the Korean

War as an assistant communications officer. The ship took part in the bombardment of enemy forces during the amphibious assault at Inchon, one of the most successful operations of the war.

The Marine Corps also recognized that it needed skilled men of all races to fight efficiently the difficult war in Korea. As a result, on 13 December 1951, Marine Corps headquarters issued a memorandum directing subordinate commands to fill all billets with qualified Marines, regardless of race.

The Navy Department's fight to end racial discrimination also proceeded on the home front during the war. In one instance, a group in Washington, D.C., which had previously sponsored social events for servicemen and government

employees, arranged a cruise on the Potomac River exclusively for whites. Learning of the group's insistence on racial segregation, local commanders removed notices posted on government property advertising the event and pulled passes that would have enabled white Sailors to attend. The official response formally declining the invitation pointed out that the Department of Defense disapproved of the staging of racially segregated activities. On 10 November 1950, the Navy Department's Chief of Information, who monitored civilian-sponsored social events, issued a Navywide letter of instruction advising that "all commands should be guided by a policy of avoidance of official participation or in furtherance of the sponsorship

NH 96903

Crewmen transfer 8-inch powder charges to the heavy cruiser Toledo *(CA 133) from a barge alongside, at Sasebo, Japan. That year* Toledo's *guns destroyed enemy targets ashore during the Inchon amphibious landing and later operations on the east coast of North Korea. The warship completed two more Korean War tours.*

of any entertainment which is racially discriminatory in nature."

Late in 1950, Clarence Mitchell Jr., director of the Washington Bureau of the National Association of Colored People (NAACP), proposed two apparently simple actions designed to further equal treatment and opportunity within the Navy and also signal civilian communities that the service remained committed to racial integration. The civil rights organization wanted the

Navy first to stop using the standard racial identifiers—Caucasian, Mongolian, Negroid, Indian (American), and Malaysian—on personnel files; and second, to stop the housing and messing of recruits at racially segregated motels and restaurants while the new Sailors awaited transportation to a naval installation.

Although a strong advocate of equal treatment and opportunity, Secretary Matthews rejected

Mitchell's recommendations. In some cities, especially though not exclusively in the South, there were no public accommodations that would serve blacks and whites equally. Unless a military or naval installation was near at hand, the Navy sometimes had no choice but to sign separate contracts to house and feed white and African American recruits. As for the racial labels, Matthews believed that the information was necessary to administer the program of racial integration and evaluate its results.

Even as the Navy struggled with segregation in the United States, L. Alex Wilson, a correspondent for the *Chicago Defender*, surveyed the state of racial integration within naval forces in Korea. Wilson found that the African Americans with whom he talked believed that the Navy was truly committed to racial integration and that the treatment they received was improving. Race relations, they said, were more harmonious at sea than in port, for ashore alcohol tended to dissolve personal inhibitions and the bonds of naval discipline. Despite the occasional brawl fueled by strong drink, a sizable number of whites seemed willing to associate with blacks and support equal treatment and opportunity—or at least not oppose the policy—and they served as a stabilizing influence on race relations.

The whites whom Wilson interviewed seemed to fall into three groups: a "fair percentage" accepted racial integration; a middle group was willing to go along with current policy; a minority felt that black Sailors were receiving unfair preferential treatment. Wilson believed that persuading this last

Clarence Mitchell, director of the Washington Bureau of the NAACP, advised the Navy in late 1950 to take further steps to promote equal opportunity in the service.

group to accept, if not embrace, equal treatment and opportunity required strong leadership from officers and petty officers. Not every naval leader shared this commitment, Wilson reported, but even those who did not realized that they had to go along with Navy policy, for the sake of their careers.

Another representative of the black press, Collins George of the *Pittsburgh Courier*, was much less optimistic than Wilson. In May 1951, he painted a discouraging picture of race relations at Camp Lejeune, North Carolina, and the adjacent town of Jacksonville. He described a "surface integration" beneath which "a deep core of old-fashioned segregation still festers." In his opinion, this ingrained racism influenced relations among Marines and affected the assignment of family housing.

After reviewing George's article, officers of the Division of Plans and Policies at Marine Corps headquarters responded promptly and vigorously. They disputed his assertion that black families lived in quarters inferior to those assigned to whites. They observed, "Negro Marines, white Marines, and their families have identical living quarters on a Marine Corps post or station." The officers acknowledged that segregation and racial discrimination did exist, however, in the town of Jacksonville, where federally administered housing projects reflected local law and custom, which codified white supremacy.

The Marine leaders of the Division of Plans and Policies believed, moreover, that official policy could go just so far in governing relations between blacks and whites who wore the uniform. They observed, "[T]he choice of friends, companions, and associates is an individual right of each Marine and cannot be directed by anyone." The racial prejudice that George dis-covered "can be eliminated only by the individual, which takes time. . . . Legislation and directives cannot do this job."

Despite the obvious problems, the Navy Department accomplished a great deal during the Korean War era. The policy of equal treatment and opportunity resulted in the more efficient use of manpower. Service men and women were being trained and assigned to specialties that fit their abilities. Refusing to cooperate with sponsors of racially segregated

As Under Secretary of the Navy and after 31 July 1951 as Secretary of the Navy, Dan A. Kimball was instrumental in carrying out reforms recommended by the Fahy Committee. In particular, he worked to improve racial integration in the Navy and to provide more training for blacks in the radar, gunnery, and engineering ratings.

Stewards, in traditional work attire, man a chow line on board the battleship Wisconsin *(BB 63), then operating off Korea. During the early 1950s, the Navy encouraged African American Sailors to qualify for other billets that had been opened to them.*

social or recreational events did not generate serious opposition from Sailors and Marines or from prospective sponsors.

Evolution of the Steward Branch

One problem persisted—racial integration of the Navy's Steward Branch, the percentage of blacks having remained fairly constant throughout the Korean War. Lester Granger, executive director of the National Urban League, called attention as early as the autumn of 1952 to the static racial composition of the Steward Branch. Granger asked Secretary of the Navy Dan Kimball to comment on "allegations"—which Granger knew were wildly exaggerated—that "90% of Negro personnel in the

Stewards in carrier Valley Forge *(CV 45) deployed off Korea attend shipboard classes to broaden their skills and enable them to qualify for other ratings.*

Navy" continued to serve in that specialty. When the Secretary of the Navy was tardy in providing accurate statistics, another request followed. This time, a search of Navy records revealed that 65 percent of the stewards were African American. "Although this percentage may appear high to you," Kimball conceded, "you must know . . . that a marked change has taken place since 1945," when Granger had served as an aide to Secretary Forrestal. Despite progress with integration, however, it was clear that the make-up of the Steward Branch was proving to be a difficult problem for the Navy.

The continued concentration of African Americans in the Steward Branch also caught the attention of New York Representative Adam Clayton Powell. "Will you be kind enough to advise me," he asked an assistant secretary of the Navy, "why your office continues to assign

This seaman ignores the cold and falling snow, so characteristic of the harsh Korean winters, to repair the 40-millimeter antiaircraft gun on board the aircraft carrier **Princeton** *(CV 37).*

NA 80-G-422343

The graduates of Stewards Class No. 3007 proudly pose for their group photo in April 1953 at Great Lakes Naval Training Station. Not only did the Navy work to integrate black Sailors into most ratings but to integrate white Sailors into the predominantly black Steward Branch.

NA 80-G-483529

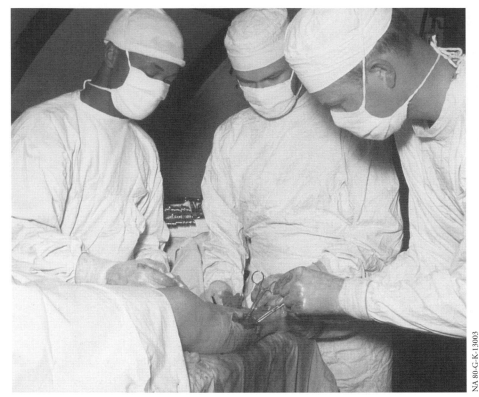

Navy personnel, part of a naval medical battalion supporting Marine ground forces at Munsan-ni in South Korea, operate on the leg of a Marine wounded in heavy fighting during September 1952.

roughly one half of the Negroes in the United States Navy to work as messmen?" This apportionment of African American manpower, still taking place as the Korean War drew to an end, suggested to Powell that black Sailors were "fighting communism with a frying pan or shoe polish."

Powell's sarcasm not withstanding, there were several factors that influenced the racial composition of the Steward Branch. In addition to tradition, many African Americans gravitated to this branch of the Navy because of the potential for long-term employment and promotion. The fact that the Steward Branch reenlistment rate historically hovered around 80 percent at least partly reflected job satisfaction. In addition, the low test scores of many African American recruits, often the product of poor, underfunded primary and sec-

A light machine gun squad from Company D, 3d Battalion, 1st Marines moves up to the front in July 1953. Like the Navy, the Marine Corps recognized that its heavy operational requirements would not allow the inefficient segregation of units. Accordingly, on 13 December 1951, Marine Corps headquarters directed commands to fill their billets with qualified Marines, regardless of race.

A USS English *(DD 696) 40-millimeter gun crew of black and white Sailors, the norm in the Navy after the Korean War, prepare to bombard enemy installations on the Korean coast.*

NA 80-G-426556

ondary schools, precluded their assignment to other job specialties in the Navy. Reality thus clashed with the interests of a Navy trying to carry out a program, based on Executive Order 9981 and approved by the Fahy Committee, to broaden opportunities for blacks through integration into the other sectors of the service.

Besides embarrassing the Navy, the racial composition of the Steward Branch convinced many African Americans outside the service that the Navy would steer blacks away from non-steward specialties. Attempts by the Navy to encourage stewards to qualify for other ratings had limited success during the war. Steward First Class Herbert Odom, who ranked first in his training class of electronics technicians, was an exception.

After the war, the Navy convened a special panel to study ways to better integrate the Steward Branch. The panel recommended against offering special incentives to induce whites to volunteer for the branch and called for an end to recruiting expressly for the Steward Branch, and proposed focusing recruiting efforts in northern cities where integrated work forces were the norm. On 28 February 1954, seven months after the armistice that ended the Korean War, the Navy decided to end all first enlistments specifically for the Steward Branch. New recruits would be exposed to the range of opportunities in the service before they could join the Steward Branch. Recruits could not volunteer for steward duty until completion of boot camp,

which gave the individual a better sense of the variety of training the Navy offered and his suitability for the different specialties.

This and other measures eventually resulted in a demographic change of the Steward Branch. More Filipino, Chamorro, and white Americans joined the branch so that by 1956, only 26 percent (the figure was never below 50 percent in the period from 1945 to 1955) of the Navy's stewards were African American. Moreover, between 1956 and 1961, roughly 600 black Sailors transferred in grade from the steward billet to other ratings.

Black Pioneers of the Korean War Era

The Korean War era was a watershed in the history of the racial integration of the Navy. In theory, if not always in practice, the Navy Department supported equal opportunity and treatment for Sailors of all races. At the same time, trail-blazing African Americans repeatedly demonstrated that they had much to contribute to defense of the nation, some of them, including Jesse L. Brown, sacrificing their lives. When he died in the frigid mountains of North Korea in December 1950, he was the only fully qualified African American naval aviator and one of just twenty-one black male and female officers. Other African Americans, however were ready to pick up the colors and move forward. Earl L. Carter pinned on his wings of gold in January 1951, earned a promotion to lieutenant (jg), and flew F9F Panther jets from the aircraft carrier *Bon Homme Richard* (CV 31) in

Black Sports Heroes of the Korean War Era

BLACK BOXERS ENJOYED remarkable success during the Korean War period. Kenneth J. Bryant, representing the Naval Station at Kodiak, became the heavyweight champion of the armed forces in Alaska. In the Golden Gloves amateur competition at San Diego, two boxers from the Naval Amphibious Force—welterweight Felix Franklin and middleweight Nolan Davis—won titles in their weight divisions. At Helsinki, Finland, during the summer of 1952, Hayes Edward "Ed" Sanders became Olympic heavyweight champion, winning a gold medal by defeating Sweden's Ingemar Johannson, later heavyweight champion of the world.

African American Sailors were involved in team sports. In 1951,

Baltimore police invoked the city's Jim Crow laws to prevent a game between a baseball team of black and white Sailors from *Ashland* (LSD 1) and a team of local blacks. More typical was the experience of the men of battleship *New Jersey,* which in 1950–1951 fielded an undefeated basketball team that

included one black player. The difference stemmed from the fact that the basketball team played at a naval installation. Racially integrated teams sometimes encountered problems in cities in the United States, but the Navy made it clear that it would not condone segregation in any form.

From the *New Jersey* (BB 62) Cruise Book, 1953.

New Jersey's *winning basketball team held first place for two years in the Atlantic Fleet's basketball tournament. By 1953, three black players had joined the team.*

Courtesy Naval Aviation History Branch

Lieutenant (jg) Earl L. Carter, following in the footsteps of Jesse Brown, pauses for a photo in the cockpit of his F9F Panther jet before launching from the carrier Bonhomme Richard *(CV 31) for another combat mission in Korea.*

combat operations over Korea. Ensign Albert Floyd became a naval aviator in March 1951 and served with the all-weather training unit at Naval Air Station, Key West, Florida. Second Lieutenant Frank F. Petersen Jr., the first African American Marine to become a naval aviator, earned his wings and his commission in October 1952. During the spring and summer of 1953, he flew sixty-four combat missions over Korea. Petersen retired from the Marine Corps as a lieutenant general.

The outstanding service of black Sailors in the Korean War did not end discrimination against African Americans, as demonstrated by the experience of a black officer, Ensign Louis Ivey, in the years after that conflict. A graduate of the NROTC program at Pennsylvania State University, Ivey was assigned in February 1954 to battleship *New Jersey* (BB 62), just returned to Norfolk, Virginia, from Korean waters. The night he reported on board, the black officer, the first ever to serve in *New Jersey,* shared a cabin with a white officer. For whatever reason, the next morning the white officer pulled rank and insisted Ivey find other quarters in the more spartan "ensign locker." Ivey grad-

ually made friends among the other officers as he learned his duties in the boiler division and then in communications.

Social interaction ashore in the rigidly segregated Norfolk, Virginia, of the mid-1950s was another matter. The naval officer could not accompany his shipmates to the city's theaters, bars, and restaurants. He was compelled to spend much of his off-duty time on the naval base, where he could not be denied access to officers' club and other facilities, thanks to President Truman's directive of July 1948. When he did take liberty in town, he associated mostly with the few other black officers stationed in the area, carefully observing Norfolk's discriminatory racial laws and customs.

Only once during his tour of active duty did the civilian hosts of a social event make a special effort to put him at ease. The sponsors of a dance held in Mayport, Florida, asked Ivey if he wanted them to arrange a date for him, as they were doing for unmarried white officers. He agreed, and his date turned out to be a "very, very attractive, very elegant, very super" young African American. At other similar events, he remained a presence rather than a participant.

Overseas, Ivey discovered that he could move about freely in the company of other officers, whether white or black. For example, when *New Jersey* put in at Cherbourg, France, he joined two white ensigns in a four-day visit to Paris. There they experienced none of the complications that the interracial group would have encountered in Norfolk.

Ensign Ivey soon understood that African American enlisted men were proud that one of their own had

Marine Second Lieutenant Frank E. Petersen Jr. was the fourth African American to receive the naval aviator designation. In Korea, Petersen flew F4U Corsairs with Marine Attack Squadron 212.

USMC A 347177

These Sailors—one white, one black—prepare for combat action off the coast of Korea, much as their predecessors had done throughout the history of the United States Navy.

NA 80-G-476624

become a naval officer. Ivey also realized that he was important to the black Sailors as a sympathetic listener and adviser. As an officer, he had frequent contact with African American stewards in the wardroom. He found that they served him promptly and courteously, as if to make it easier for him to cope with each day in the company of the mostly white officer complement of *New Jersey.*

Getting along with his fellow officers could be tricky, for the Navy still had a good distance to go to achieve genuine racial integration. He had to endure snubs and thoughtless jokes. He remained open to overtures of friendship from whites but was wary of making approaches of his own. Thus did he pick his way through the minefield that was race relations in the Navy, which reflected American society in general. After completing the tour of active duty required of a reserve officer commissioned through the NROTC, Ivey returned to civilian

life, entered medical school, and became a prominent surgeon.

Although the Navy in which Ivey served continued to reflect the racial prejudices of a society segregated by law and custom, the lot of the black naval officer had improved since World War II. When the first African American officers received their commissions in 1944, some white enlisted men refused to salute them. As late as the Korean War, a restaurant in Oxnard, California, refused to serve an African American officer unless he sat in isolation at a table near the kitchen; but a white officer arrived, threatened to have the business declared off-limits to naval personnel, and forced the owner to relent. The Navy and the other armed forces, by carrying out President Truman's policy of equal treatment and opportunity, had moved ahead of a civilian society inching even more slowly toward racial integration.

The Navy's progress in race relations reflected Executive Order

9981, the work of the Fahy Committee, and the manpower needs of the Korean War. During the decade following that conflict, the concentration of blacks in the Steward Branch at last ended. Blacks in the enlisted force nevertheless totaled only about 5 percent during the post-World War II period. The officer corps of the Navy of 1962 included 174 African Americans; men and women, regulars and reservists.

These figures represented definite improvement over pre-World War II and wartime totals, but they also demonstrated that the African American community remained a neglected national resource. Tragically, the United States would have to endure courtroom battles, urban rioting, other social and political upheavals, and dissention in the armed forces during the 1960s and 1970s before African Americans could become fully contributing members of the U.S. Navy.

Acknowledgments

I am grateful to Dr. Edward J. Marolda for the opportunity to write this account and for his editorial guidance and that of the Center's staff, especially Dr. Regina Akers and Ms. Sandra Doyle. I fear that Dr. Marolda discovered, as other editors have, that, when asked the time of day, I tend to respond with an essay on watch-making.

Paul Stillwell of the U.S. Naval Institute, and the staff of that organization's library, earned my gratitude by making available to me the transcripts of his interviews with African American officers of the Korean War era.

The Navy Department Library generously shared its holdings, including issues of *Our Navy* and *All Hands: The Bureau of Naval Personnel Information Bulletin,* which contain items revealing the changing role and greater acceptance of African American Sailors during the 1950s.

About the Author

Bernard Nalty spent almost forty years as a government historian, contributing during his career to the *History of U.S. Marine Corps Operations in World War II* and to the Air Force's official history of the Vietnam War. In the field of Black History, he collaborated with Morris J. MacGregor in editing the 13-volume *Blacks in the United States Armed Forces: Basic Documents* and its one-volume abridgement, *Blacks in the Military: Essential Documents.* He also wrote *Strength for the Fight: A History of Black Americans in the Military* and *The Right to Fight: African American Marines in World War II,* the latter a pamphlet in a series published by the Marine Corps to commemorate its contributions to victory in World War II.

Sources

Document Collections

MacGregor, Morris J., Jr., and Bernard C. Nalty, eds. *Blacks in the United States Armed Forces: Basic Documents,* 13 volumes. Wilmington, DE: Scholarly Resources, 1977.

Interviews by Paul Stillwell, U.S. Naval Institute, Annapolis, MD.
Commander Wesley A. Brown, 1986.
Vice Admiral Samuel A. Gravely Jr., 1986.
Commander John Wesley Lee Jr. (published by Naval Institute Press, 1994).

General Surveys

Astor, Gerald. *The Right to Fight: A History of African Americans in the Military.* Novato, CA: Presidio Press, 1998.

Foner, Jack D. *Blacks and the Military in American History: A New Perspective.* New York: Praeger, reprint 1974.

Nalty, Bernard C. *Strength for the Fight: A History of Black Americans in the Military.* New York: The Free Press, 1986.

Books

Altoff, Gerald. *Amongst My Best Men: African Americans and the War of 1812.* Put-in-Bay, OH: The Perry Group, 1996.

Bolster, W. Jeffrey. *Black Jacks: African American Seamen in the Age of Sail.* Cambridge, MA: Harvard University Press, 1997.

Gould, William B., IV. *Diary of a Contraband: The Civil War Passage of a Black Sailor.* Palo Alto: Stanford University Press, 2002.

Harrod, Frederick S. *Manning the New Navy: The Development of a Modern Naval Enlisted Force, 1899–1940.* Westport, CT: Greenwood Press, 1978.

MacGregor, Morris J., Jr. *Defense Studies Series: Integration of the Armed Forces, 1940–1965.*

Washington: Center of Military History, 1981.

Nelson, Dennis D. *The Integration of the Negro into the U.S. Navy.* New York: Octagon Books, reprint, 1982.

Ramold, Steven J. *Slaves, Sailors, Citizens: African Americans in the Union Navy.* Dekalb: Northern Illinois University Press, 2002.

Shaw, Henry I., Jr., and Ralph W. Donnelly. *Blacks in the Marine Corps.* Washington: History and Museums Division, Headquarters, U.S. Marine Corps, reprint, 1988.

Stillwell, Paul. *Battleship New Jersey: An Illustrated History.* Annapolis, MD: Naval Institute Press, reprint 1989. Recounts the experiences of a newly commissioned African American officer during the mid-1950s.

_____. *The Golden Thirteen: Recollections of the First Black Naval Officers.* Annapolis, MD: Naval Institute Press, 1993.

Taylor, Theodore. *The Flight of Jesse Leroy Brown.* New York: Avon Books, 1998.

Uya, Okun Edet. *From Slavery to Public Service: Robert Smalls, 1839–1915.* New York: Oxford University Press, 1977.

Articles

Bolster, W. Jeffrey. " 'To Feel Like a Man': Black Seamen in the Northern States." *Journal of American History* (March 1990).

Brewer, Charles C. "African American Sailors and the Unvexing of the Mississippi River." *Prologue: Quarterly of the National Archives and Records Administration* (Winter 1998).

Harrod, Frederick S. "Integration of the Navy (1941–1978)." U.S. Naval Institute *Proceedings* (October 1979).

_____. "Jim Crow in the Navy (1798–1941)." U.S. Naval Institute *Proceedings* (September 1979).

Langley, Harold D. "The Negro in the Navy and Merchant Service, 1798–1860." *Journal of Negro History* (October 1969).

Logan, Rayford W. "The Negro in the Quasi War, 1798–1800." *Negro History Bulletin* (March 1951).

Miller, Richard E. "A Yachtsman's Tale." *All Hands* (February 1988).

_____. "The Golden Fourteen, Plus: Black Women in World War One." *Minerva: Quarterly Report of Women and the Military* 13 (Fall/Winter, 1995).

Reidy, Joseph P. "Black Jack: African American Sailors in the Civil War Navy." In *New Interpretations in Naval History: Selected Papers from the Twelfth Naval History Symposium.* Annapolis, MD: Naval Institute Press, 1997.

Weems, John E. "Black Wings of Gold." U.S. Naval Institute *Proceedings* (July 1983).

ISBN 0-16-051355-3